LEARNING VITAL READING STRATEGIES

A Workbook for Students

Amelia Leighton Gamel

Supplement to the Instructor Text,
Help! My College Students Can't Read

ROWMAN & LITTLEFIELD
Lanham • Boulder • New York • London

Published by Rowman & Littlefield
A wholly owned subsidiary of The Rowman & Littlefield Publishing Group, Inc.
4501 Forbes Boulevard, Suite 200, Lanham, Maryland 20706
www.rowman.com

Unit A, Whitacre Mews, 26-34 Stannary Street, London SE11 4AB

Copyright © 2016 by Amelia Leighton Gamel

ISBN 978-1-4758-2223-6 (paperback : alk. paper)
ISBN 978-1-4758-2224-3 (ebook)

All rights reserved. No part of this book may be reproduced in any form or by any electronic or mechanical means, including information storage and retrieval systems, without written permission from the publisher, except by a reviewer who may quote passages in a review.

∞™ The paper used in this publication meets the minimum requirements of American National Standard for Information Sciences—Permanence of Paper for Printed Library Materials, ANSI/NISO Z39.48-1992.

Printed in the United States of America

LEARNING
VITAL READING
STRATEGIES

CONTENTS

	INTRODUCTION	vii
1	**ACTIVE READING**	1
	Reading Strategies	1
2	**DETERMINING A PURPOSE**	3
	Making Predictions	3
	Determining a Purpose	5
	Evaluating Possible Purposes	6
	Ways to Stay Engaged While Reading	7
3	**DETERMINING WHAT'S IMPORTANT**	9
	Striking Out Unneeded Information	9
4	**DEVELOPING HIGHER-LEVEL QUESTIONS**	15
	Focus Quadrants	15
	Asking Questions as We Read	18
5	**MAKING CONNECTIONS**	21
	Drawing Inferences	21
	Connecting to Prior Knowledge	24
6	**NAVIGATING UNKNOWN WORDS**	27
	Dealing with Difficult Vocabulary	27
	Pie Chart Vocabulary	28
	Ways to Study Lists of Terms	29

CONTENTS

7	**CREATING VISUALS TO ENHANCE COMPREHENSION AND RECALL**	31
	Practice Creating Visuals	31
8	**KEEPING IT REAL**	35
	Professional Spotlight Interviews	35
	Conduct Your Own Professional Reading Interview	42

INTRODUCTION

WHY YOU NEED THIS WORKBOOK

If you have been assigned this workbook, you have an instructor who knows how important strong reading skills are to success in your education and in your career. That instructor also knows that more and more students are entering college unprepared for the challenges of college-level reading.

Many factors play a part in this, such as K–12 educational systems, socioeconomics, and family dynamics. Technology is also adding to the problem. People are becoming more and more accustomed to short pieces of information and to quickly clicking away that information if it is not interesting or is hard to understand. This can make it difficult to effectively focus on college-level academic material.

The reality for many students, even relatively strong readers, is that they need strategies to navigate college texts and to actively engage with the material in them. Engaged readers are more able to comprehend information and to remember and use that information.

This workbook contains activities to help you learn to be a more engaged reader. These activities directly relate to in-class lessons on reading strategies from the instructor's edition and provide opportunities for you to practice what you are learning.

Three actions are necessary for learning a new skill. We need to hear the process of that skill explained, see the skill performed by someone else, and then practice the skill ourselves. The same is true with reading strategies. You will

INTRODUCTION

need to hear the strategies explained by your instructor, watch as your instructor shows you how they work, then practice the strategies for yourself as you read.

This workbook offers many opportunities for such practice. It is a workbook meant to be worked. Mark up the pages, create your own visual images, fill the margins with notes and questions. Let this workbook help you learn to engage with what you're reading. Let it be a training ground to become an active and strategic college reader.

HOW THIS WORKBOOK IS ORGANIZED

Each chapter begins with a quote and a "Point to Ponder" to engage your brain in thinking about the concepts that will be covered. In most chapters, this will be followed by exercises and activities to help you become a stronger reader.

Chapter 1 provides a list of active reading strategies. If you are like many students, you might not be sure what it means to be an "active reader." When you hear about it in your college classroom, the concept will be brand new to you. Or like other students, you will have some idea about and maybe even some experience with active reading, but it will not be something you intentionally practice, especially with academic texts.

Chapters 2 through 7 each focus on specific reading strategies your instructor might choose to teach you in class. Many engaging activities, exercises, and other resources are provided to get you personally involved in the act of learning to be a stronger reader. These are designed to be done in the classroom along with your instructor and other students or on your own outside of class.

In chapter 8, the last chapter of the workbook, you will find two "Professional Spotlight Interviews." These contain a photo of a professional person, the person's job title, and an interview that highlights how vital it is for someone in that particular field to have strong reading skills. The purpose is to demonstrate that knowing how to read well is not just something you need to get a college diploma, but something you need to be successful in your future career. Following this is a list of questions you can use to conduct your own professional reading interview. This will help you find out how important reading skills are in career fields you might want to pursue.

THE BOTTOM LINE

On campuses everywhere, students are walking into their classes without the reading skills they need to face the challenges of college-level texts.

INTRODUCTION

Whatever factors have played into this (K–12 education, socioeconomics, family dynamics, the impact of technology, or any number of other things), the reality is that if you are one of those students who cannot effectively navigate academic material, you will find it very difficult to adequately comprehend the information you encounter, to remember it, learn it, or put it to use.

That's the bad news. The good news is the strategies in this workbook will help you develop the strong reading skills you need. But you must choose to learn these strategies, practice them, and use them with intentional focus as you read your academic texts. This will take dedication, but the payoffs can be huge. Learning to be an effective reader can not only help you be successful in college, but can increase your ability to be successful in whatever career field you choose.

ACTIVE READING

Tell me and I forget, teach me and I may remember, involve me and I learn.
—Benjamin Franklin

> **Point to ponder:** Think about how reading strategies help you get the most information out of your reading in the least amount of time.

READING STRATEGIES

- Look at the title, section headings, and so forth and predict what the text might be about.
- Determine a purpose for reading (what you want to know or what the author wants you to know).
- Think through what you already know about the topic of the text before you start reading. As you read, connect new information you encounter to information you have already learned from other sources, life experiences, and so on.
- As you read, underline words, phrases, or sentences that directly relate to your purpose. If any ideas come to your mind about why this information is important, jot them down.
- While reading, strike through unnecessary words or phrases that are not directly related to your purpose. For more on this strategy, see chapter 3.

- Jot down specific questions that come to mind as you read, then look for answers as you continue. Note: one-word questions such as "How?" or "Why?" are not specific enough to be helpful.
- Create visuals such as drawings, charts, diagrams, or timelines to help you remember concepts, steps in a process, sequences of events, and so on as you encounter them in the reading.
- Jot down a short summary or bulleted list of information at least once per page.
- Look up definitions of unknown words or use other strategies to discover word meanings. Such strategies could be identifying parts of the word you already know (roots, prefixes, or suffixes), determining if the word sounds or looks like another word you do know, or looking for context clues to help you figure out possible meanings.

2

DETERMINING A PURPOSE

What we see depends mainly on what we're looking for.

—Anonymous

> **Point to ponder:** Think about how making predictions and having a purpose for reading will help you effectively focus on the information you are looking for and will make the information seem to jump off the page.

MAKING PREDICTIONS

Develop a prediction and a specific reading purpose for the textbook titles below and for each chapter title listed from these textbooks. Remember, a prediction is a guess of what you think the text will be about. A reading purpose is what you specifically want to know or what the author specifically wants you to know from the text.

Textbook title: *Medical Law and Ethics*

Prediction

_____

Purpose

_____

Chapter 3 title: "Importance of the Legal System for the Physician and the Healthcare Professional"

Prediction

_____

Purpose

_____

Chapter 6 title: "Professional Liability and Medical Malpractice"

Prediction

_____

Purpose

_____

Textbook title: *Sonography: Introduction to Normal Structure and Function*

Prediction

_____

Purpose

_____

Chapter 1 title: "Before and After the Ultrasound Examination"

Prediction

_____

Purpose

_____

Textbook title: *Psychology*

Prediction

_____

Purpose

_____

Chapter 12 title: "Emotions, Stress, and Health"

Prediction

_____

Purpose

_____

I hope to learn more about the benefits of brain testing and the
advantages it offers.   _____

I am curious about the new test.   _____

About brain tests and diagnosis.   _____

About the different kinds of brain tests.   _____

WAYS TO STAY ENGAGED WHILE READING

- Try to understand new information by connecting it to something you already know. (If you're reading about how the voting system works in another country, make connections to what you know about how voting works in your country.)
- Visualize characters, settings, concepts, processes, sequences, and so forth. (If you are reading about a process that has nine steps, picture a train with nine cars sitting on a railroad track. Imagine each car with a picture on the side that helps you remember one of the steps.)
- Ask yourself questions as you read, and then look for the answers. (If you read that Mark Zuckerberg was one of five cofounders of Facebook, ask yourself what part he played, then read on to see if the text describes his role.)
- Mark up a text as you read. (Underline important information, highlight unknown words or unfamiliar phrases, circle important verbs, cross out irrelevant material, restate information in bullet form.)
- Compare or contrast things. (If you are reading about how the human brain works, think about how a brain and a computer are alike or different.)
- Think about how other viewpoints are different from yours. (If you are reading about the death penalty and are against it, think about how you might feel differently if you were in the shoes of someone whose loved one was murdered.)
- Analyze a problem or situation. (If you are reading about the problem of high illiteracy rates among people living in poverty, think about what might have caused this problem and try to come up with possible solutions.)
- Evaluate information. (If you are reading about two studies on the effects of video games on children, one that gives negative results and one that gives positive results, evaluate the quality and sources of the information to decide which study is the most credible.)

REFERENCES

Curry, R. A., and B. B. Tempkin. 2011. *Sonography: Introduction to Normal Structure and Function*. 3rd ed. St. Louis, MO: Saunders.
Fremgen, B. F. 2012. *Medical Law and Ethics*. 4th ed. Upper Saddle River, NJ: Pearson.
Myers, D. G. 2010. *Psychology*. 9th ed. New York: Worth.

3

DETERMINING WHAT'S IMPORTANT

Readers of nonfiction have to decide and remember what is important in the texts they read if they are going to learn anything from them.

—Stephanie Harvey and Anne Goudvis

> **Point to ponder:** Think about how determining what's important when you read helps you focus on vital information and keeps you from being distracted by irrelevant and unnecessary details.

STRIKING OUT UNNEEDED INFORMATION

Below are directions and an article for an activity using the strategy of striking out unneeded information.

DIRECTIONS: Using the title and section headings of the article, make predictions about the topic of the article and develop a purpose for reading it. Remember, one way to develop a purpose is to think about what you want to know from the reading or what you think the author wants you to know. Write your responses on the lines below.

Prediction

_____

_____

CHAPTER 3

Purpose

_____

_____

Next read through the article and strike out any material that does not directly pertain to your purpose. Leave only the specific information that you determine is important and that supports your purpose for reading the article. Determining what is needed and striking out what isn't requires differentiating between three types of information you will encounter:

- information that is important and relates to your purpose for reading;
- information that is interesting but doesn't relate to your purpose for reading;
- information that is neither important nor interesting and doesn't relate to your purpose for reading.

 Readers generally have little difficulty with the first and third types of information because the relevance or lack of relevance to their purpose is easy to determine. However, they have more trouble with the second type. When readers encounter interesting information, their attention is drawn to it, and they have a more difficult time determining what they should strike out. When this happens, think through the information carefully to determine if it is directly related to your purpose for reading. If it isn't, strike it out.

 Remember, striking out information doesn't mean it's not important. It just means it's not relevant to a reader's focused purpose. If it's not relevant, it's not needed. Getting unneeded material out of the way makes it easier to focus on what's left. For instance, in the introduction, you might consider striking out everything except "Shifts in public policy, a lack of mental health services, and inadequate parole supervision are serious contributing factors to the high recidivism rates."

 When you have finished working through the article striking out what isn't relevant to your purpose, go back and read what you have left. It will be easy to see how this strategy allows you to locate what is important in a text and to focus on what is specific to your purpose. This strategy also makes studying for tests and quizzes much easier because it eliminates the need to read a lot of unnecessary material and keeps you from getting distracted by irrelevant details.

"FACTORS LEADING TO INCREASED RECIDIVISM RATES OF MENTALLY ILL PAROLEES" BY KIERNAN GAMEL

A major mental health policy issue is the recidivism rate of mentally ill parolees. Shifts in public policy, a lack of mental health services, and inadequate parole supervision are serious contributing factors to the high recidivism rates among this underserved segment of the mentally ill population. As a result, growing numbers of offenders with mental illness are repeatedly cycling through correctional systems across the country.

Shifts in Public Policy

Shifts in public policy have had a major impact on the recidivism rates of individuals suffering from mental illness. One such policy shift involved de-institutionalizing the mentally ill. This resulted in individuals who suffered from mental illness being systematically moved out of state public mental hospitals. From 1955 to 1980, the resident population in those facilities fell from half a million to just over 150,000.

In the 1990s, institutions began to close in significant numbers. Many leaders in the psychiatric community argued that moving patients out of state hospitals and into community-based outpatient settings represented a humane alternative to overcrowded and understaffed institutions. Unfortunately, in most cases the closing of state hospitals was not accompanied by the promised number of clinics and halfway houses necessary to care for released hospital patients. One result was a rise in the number of those with mental illness becoming involved with the criminal justice system and eventually prison.

Another public policy shift that had a major impact on the mentally ill was the anti-drug campaign during the Nixon and Reagan years. This campaign, popularly known as the "war on drugs," drew on Nancy Reagan's coined phrase "just say no" and set the stage for zero tolerance policies concerning drug use. These zero tolerance laws surrounding drug use made those with mental illness especially vulnerable to involvement with the criminal justice system due to the high prevalence of substance misuse among the mentally ill, especially those with schizophrenia or bipolar disorders. This shift in policy also led to greater numbers of the mentally ill entering the prison system.

Lack of Mental Health Services

While in prison, many mentally ill inmates do not receive any mental health care. If they do receive treatment, it typically consists of a very brief psychiatric evaluation and a medication regimen. Ongoing therapy is seldom offered. When it is offered, such treatment is often ineffective because mentally ill inmates tend to distrust mental health workers who are employed by prison systems.

When inmates with mental illness are paroled, they often face difficult challenges that put them at risk for failure. One of these is limited access to medication. Often those who suffer from mental illness and have been on psychotropic medication are released from prison with a thirty-day supply of these medications and have no means to obtain refills. When the medication is gone, the parolees soon begin another cycle of emotional and mental instability, leading to parole violations and return to prison.

Not only do they lack the ability to obtain medication, they do not have easy access to other mental health care. In many cases, the main criterion used to decide who qualifies for mental health services is the degree to which a person is considered an imminent danger to self or others. Many parolees showing up for services at mental health clinics do not meet this criterion. As a result, they are seldom seen. Instead, they are referred to local medical clinics that have no specialization in treating mental health disorders and lack the government funding needed to supply such treatment.

Even if such services were available, parolees often cannot access them because of a lack of transportation. Many do not have a valid driver's license and do not have money for public transportation or even to purchase a bicycle. This not only prevents them from getting mental health care, but also makes it very difficult for them to participate in other social supports such as Alcoholics Anonymous or Narcotics Anonymous.

Inadequate Parole Supervision

Another factor that affects overall recidivism rates for the mentally ill is the role played by parole agents. They are a major part of the system designed to assist former inmates. However, parole agents are not always equipped to help those with mental illness. Two reasons for this are their enormous caseloads and the fact that they are not specifically trained to deal with the problems faced by the mentally ill. Consequently many parolees with mental illness are not monitored effectively, which adds to the likelihood that they will discontinue their medication (if they have any to begin with) and begin to experience symptoms of their disorders.

Also, as the size of the overall parole population has grown, the ways in which parole agents manage their caseloads has gone from a traditional re-entry facilitator approach to a more surveillance-oriented and punitive approach. Parole agents are also more likely to have a law enforcement background and embrace a control model of parole supervision that focuses more on surveillance and detection and less on treatment and rehabilitation.

Conclusion

Shifts in public policy, a lack of mental health services, and inadequate parole supervision have created a devastating cycle for many with mental illness. Those who have no safety net, such as family to care for them, find it very difficult to effectively integrate into society. As a result, they end up on a merry-go-round of crisis interventions, hospitalizations, homelessness, and repeated incarceration. This is a major issue in mental health policy that must be addressed to prevent the endless recycling of the mentally ill through America's correctional systems.

4

DEVELOPING HIGHER-LEVEL QUESTIONS

The art and science of asking questions is the source of all knowledge.

—Thomas Berger

> **Point to ponder:** Consider how focusing on higher-level questions helps you become a better reader and a better thinker.

FOCUS QUADRANTS

The human brain learns to think best when it is challenged with good questions, ones that require more than simple "yes or no" responses, ones that require us to move from lower levels of thinking to higher levels of thinking. That is why it is important to develop such questions for ourselves as we read.

Reading is a skill that requires more than visually processing words. It requires mentally processing words, making meaning out of them, and then thinking critically about that meaning. Asking yourself higher-level questions (meaty questions that require serious thinking) as you read helps you interact with a text on a deeper level, which makes you not only a better reader, but a better thinker. The following exercise will give you practice at developing higher-level questions.

Look carefully at the photographs in the exercise, then create a list of no fewer than five higher-level questions in each category of the quadrant below each picture. Remember, these questions should require more than simple "yes or no" responses. Some sample questions have been provided in the quadrant below the leaf picture to get you started.

Figure 4.1. Leaf of Life. *Photographer: Dudley Campfield, 2014*

Environmental	Physiological
How does the process of photosynthesis tie in with current environmental issues?	How does photosynthesis contribute to the life of human beings?
Political	**Biological**
What steps can the government take to ensure sustainability of woodlands?	How can the energy of photosynthesis be harnessed to aid in cell growth or development?

DEVELOPING HIGHER-LEVEL QUESTIONS

Historical	Environmental
Chemical	**Technological**

17

CHAPTER 4

ASKING QUESTIONS AS WE READ

Humans constantly seek to understand the world by asking questions. Think about how many times you ask yourself questions in a day. How many times in an hour? How many times in a minute? Our senses are taking in so much information that we have a constant stream of questions going through our minds, nearly unconsciously sometimes: Who's wearing that strong perfume? I wonder where that ambulance I just heard is going. Why is it so hot in here? What do I want for lunch? What's written on the back of that guy's T-shirt?

We can consciously use this natural inclination while we are reading. The key word here is "consciously." Whether we are fully aware of it or not, our minds are asking all kinds of questions as we read. We just need to slow our minds down enough to consciously focus on them.

A good way to do this is to start paying attention to how many times our brains say "Hmm?" as we read. It's that little pause right before a question comes. Hmm? What does that mean? Hmm? Why would they say that? Hmm? How does that work?

Once we start noticing when our brains pause to say "Hmm?" we can pause to consciously focus on the question that is coming. For instance, if we are reading an article about homelessness and read that it is a rapidly growing problem among younger military veterans, our brains are likely to say, "Hmm, I wonder why that is." We can then focus on that question by jotting it down and then looking for the answer as we continue reading.

In the following exercise, you can practice consciously focusing on the "Hmm?" pauses that happen inside your head. Read the story below. Each time you sense a "Hmm?" pause, stop and think about the question that is forming in your mind and jot it in the margin. Then as you continue to read, every time you find possible answers to those questions, jot them in the margin as well.

"THE DELIVERY WOMAN" BY RHONDA HURST

The woman stood outside the man's door with a key in her hand. They had lived a long time in the same run-down apartment building, she on the bottom floor and he on the top. Nearly every day for the last ten years, she had gone up the four flights of stairs to his flat and left things outside his door. Groceries, mail, things like that. Two times a month, there would also be a bundle of newspapers. It would show up at the post office all wrapped in plastic and bound with twine.

She had decided that the papers were from places he went on his trips. He was always gone twice a month, and the bundles always came a few days after he got back. She couldn't ask him because they never talked except in notes left on doors. It had been like that since the first day they met.

That had been out on the front sidewalk. He had taken his umbrella to two tough boys who, for sport, had knocked a shopping bag out of her hands. "The powerful must be brought low!" he had repeated along with the blows. Those were the only words she had ever heard him say. When the boys fled, he picked up her things and carried them in. She remembered how he had silently looked around at her place. It made her feel the shabbiness of it. The next day, the first note appeared on her door. He would pay her rent if she would start the deliveries and never talk about the arrangement with anyone. That worked out. No one in the building ever talked to her anyway.

She knew the deliveries had saved her. She thought of that every time she carried things up. This has saved me, she would say to herself no matter how tired she got. The papers made her the most tired. She would have to stop and rest on the third floor landing. It was worse in the summer. The narrow stairwell was airless. There were no windows, and the door to the one fire escape had been bolted shut to keep out thieves. But those newspapers had saved her, she'd always say to herself.

Not long after the man left on his last trip, a letter arrived addressed to her in care of the man's post office box. It was from a lawyer's office. There was a key inside and a sealed note from the man.

The note was short just like all the others. He wouldn't be coming back, it said. Not for at least twenty years. Arrangements had been made for her to have his apartment and everything in it. There would be another note for her on his kitchen table.

She put the key in the door, went in, and locked the door behind her. The front hall was long and narrow, just like hers. But this one was lined on both sides with neatly stacked bundles of newspapers. She had to turn sideways to make her way through. She had never been in this flat, but it was familiar, living room to the left, bedroom and bathroom to the right, kitchen down the hall at the end, just like hers. The shades were down. She didn't raise them. She turned on some lights instead. In every room, there were more bundles of newspapers, stacked against walls and on most of the furniture.

She found the note on the table on top of another bundle. There were only two sentences. "Open them all. Start with this one." She got a knife from a drawer and cut away the twine and the plastic. The papers were from Detroit. The headline on the top one was bold. DOWNTOWN BANK ROBBED. When the woman opened the pages, money started falling out, big bills, fifties and hundreds. They fluttered to the floor in every direction faster than the woman could catch them. She opened paper after paper. More money fell onto the table, the chairs, and the floor. She ran from room to room opening bundles.

CHAPTER 4

There were papers from city after city, all with stories of bank robberies and all lined with money.

    The woman went back to the kitchen and sat down at the table. The apartment was quiet. She could hear the light over her head buzzing. It would probably quit working sooner or later, like so many other lights in the old building. A toilet flushed next door. The neighbors wouldn't notice he was gone, she thought. And they wouldn't notice if she moved in. For years they had just walked around her when she left things outside in the hallway. She should call the police, she told herself. She was just the delivery woman. They wouldn't blame her. She thought about that for a minute. That's all she had ever been, a delivery woman.

MAKING CONNECTIONS

Inference is a statement about the unknown made on the basis of the known.

—S. I. Hayakawa

> **Point to ponder:** Think about how making connections as you read helps you learn more effectively.

DRAWING INFERENCES

Imagine you are driving home and you notice one of your friends has been pulled over on the shoulder of the road by a police officer. Both are outside of their vehicles. Your friend is standing straight up, with legs together and eyes closed, facing the officer. Both of your friend's arms are outstretched at the side, with one bent at the elbow, poised to attempt a nose touch.

What do you infer is taking place?

_____
_____
_____
_____

CHAPTER 5

Think about why the officer wouldn't need to yell out to you, "I suspect this person has been drinking, and I'm facilitating a sobriety test." You could deduce this on your own by using evidence and personal knowledge to draw a reasonable conclusion. In other words, you could infer it. An inference is a conclusion reached on the basis of perceived evidence or from premises known or assumed to be true. It involves reasoning, presuming, supposing, and guessing.

Drawing inferences as we read is an effective way to connect with important information in a text. The following exercise will let you practice this skill. Each of the sentences in the case study below has been numbered. As you read through the study, stop at each sentence in bold and think about what you can infer from that sentence about the people, situations, and so forth that are being discussed. Write your inferences on the numbered lines below the case study. Some possible inferences about sentence 3 have been provided as an example. As you read, think about how inferring helps you to connect to the case study on a deeper level.

MAKING CONNECTIONS CASE STUDY

1) Denise was an adult volunteer at a youth activity center when she first met Jody, a girl from a local neighborhood. 2) Jody was twelve years old at the time and had two younger brothers. 3) **They lived with their mother and a series of the mother's boyfriends.** 4) The fathers of the children were not involved in their lives.

5) **During Jody's teen years, her mother would sometimes go away for days at a time, leaving Jody to care for the two boys with the supervision of an uncle, a single man in his thirties who lived next door. 6) The children would often run out of food and miss school during those times.**

7) Protective services had been contacted on several occasions. 8) When workers came, the uncle convinced them that the children were being cared for. 9) Denise tried to check on the children herself, but Jody wouldn't let her in. 10) **She said her uncle wouldn't like it.** 11) Denise asked if he was staying with them or at his own house. 12) **Jody told her, "He comes sometimes, usually late at night."**

13) Jody left home when she was seventeen. 14) **By the time she was twenty-two, she had four children by three different fathers. 15) She would often call Denise for help with money and food. 16) When Denise went to the house, she would find it very dirty.** 17) Sometimes there would even be dog feces on the floor. 18) **The children, all under five years old, were usually very dirty too.** 19) Denise would try to help clean things up. 20) She would also bring in food.

MAKING CONNECTIONS

21) **She had stopped offering money when she found out Jody was spending it on cigarettes for various boyfriends.**

22) **One day Denise arrived and found the children alone.** 23) **Jody was two houses down with some friends.** 24) Denise talked to her when she came back, and Jody promised she wouldn't do that anymore. 25) A few months later, Denise found the children alone again. 26) It was wintertime. 27) The front door was open, and the house was cold. 28) **The children were in underwear and T-shirts and were barefooted.** 29) Two of them had dog feces between their toes.

30) The youngest, a four-month-old boy, was in a crib in a bedroom on a bare mattress with no blankets. 31) **He was wearing only a diaper, which was wet, and he was crying.** 32) Denise left a note for Jody and took the children to her house and cleaned them up. 33) Then she reluctantly called protective services. 34) A man there told her she would have to return the children to their mother until a caseworker could visit the home. 35) He said he was sorry, but it was hard to remove children without official proof of neglect. 36) **"Show me a broken arm,"** he said. **"Then we can do something."**

37) Two weeks later, Jody called Denise from the hospital. 38) **The baby had been admitted and diagnosed with failure to thrive.** 39) He weighed only eleven pounds, just four pounds over his birth weight. 40) Denise called the man she had talked to earlier and told him she thought she had a "broken arm" to report. 41) Then she went up to the hospital to sit with Jody.

42) **Someone from protective services came to the hospital that day.** 43) All the children were placed in temporary foster care. 44) Within a few years, they were all permanently removed from their mother. 45) Jody never found out that Denise was the one who called protective services. 46) She thought it was someone at the hospital.

3. <u>From sentence 3, I infer the mother was involved in a series of unstable relationships that were difficult for her and the children and had an unsettling effect on the entire family.</u>

5. _____
   _____

6. _____
   _____

10. _____
    _____

12. _____
    _____

14. _____
_____

15. _____
_____

16. _____
_____

18. _____
_____

21. _____
_____

22. _____
_____

23. _____
_____

28. _____
_____

31. _____
_____

36. _____
_____

38. _____
_____

42. _____
_____

CONNECTING TO PRIOR KNOWLEDGE

Questions in bold have been inserted after each paragraph in the short article below. Pause and think through the questions to help you make connections to your prior knowledge about some of the topics in the text.

CLASSIC SCIENTIFIC MANAGEMENT THEORY

Classic scientific management theory came about in the late 1800s and has had a great impact on American business, especially manufacturing. It is called scientific because it is based on studying work processes to increase economic effectiveness and worker productivity and to decrease waste of materials, labor, and time.

[What kinds of things are scientists normally thought to study? Genetics? Space? Medical science? What do you know about how they normally go about such study? Did it surprise you to hear that scientists studied work processes? How do you think they might have gone about this, particularly in the late 1800s? Speculate about the motives of those scientists and what might be inferred about why they conducted such studies. Inferences can also be drawn about the motives of industry leaders of that time who put the resulting principles into practice.]

The theory was initially developed in the 1880s by a man named Frederick Winslow Taylor, who began investigating labor processes of that period. Through the 1890s up to around 1910, the theory was further developed and began to have a significant impact on the manufacturing industry. Its influence peaked in the decade leading up to 1920 and then leveled out as competing theories arose. By the 1930s, the popularity of Taylor's theory had faded significantly, but its influence on industry has remained.

[Think about how the theory developed over time, peaked in influence, then faded in popularity. Think about other such theories or fads that come and go in similar ways. What can you infer about the theory from this information?]

A main aspect of classic scientific management theory is what has become known as the division of labor, in which larger tasks are divided into smaller, more specialized ones. Individual workers perform these more specialized tasks repetitively as steps in a process to develop a product or to complete a project or work assignment. Managers closely supervise workers to ensure quality and productivity.

[Access a definition of "division of labor" from your phone or other device to see how it compares to the definition in the text. Can you think of a comparison to help you remember how workers are described in the paragraph? What about worker bees or a colony of ants?]

Factory assembly lines are an obvious example of this. However, many offices, especially bureaucracies, can be organized according to this theory, with workers often in cubicles performing narrowly specified jobs overseen by various levels of management.

[Think about what you know about factory assembly lines. Also think about the word "bureaucracies." Access a definition to see how this term refers to

CHAPTER 5

government offices. To help yourself make connections, think about experiences you have had with being passed from worker to worker to complete some government process instead of having one person help you through it. Have you had these experiences at an unemployment office? Department of Motor Vehicles? Social services office?]

Whether in the factory or the office, focus tends to be on the organization as a whole rather than on the individual workers. Workers are trained to follow precise directions to complete a task. Independent thinking or decision making is not generally encouraged, nor are workers invited to give input into the company's operation. Instead, managers make decisions based on what will benefit the organization overall, such as policies that will cut costs and raise productivity levels.

[Consider the title again, "Classic Scientific Management Theory." Use this title and the wording in the final paragraph to draw inferences about the relationship between managers and workers under this system. Make comparisons to other things you know about that operate in a similar fashion. Private schools? The military?]

6

NAVIGATING UNKNOWN WORDS

We think with words; therefore to improve thinking, teach vocabulary.
—Arthur G. Draper and Gerald H. Moeller

> **Point to ponder:** Think about how having a wider vocabulary will help you gain more meaning from your educational experiences and will provide great benefits in your professional life and your personal life.

DEALING WITH DIFFICULT VOCABULARY

- What vocabulary resources can I use to help me define a word (e-devices, glossaries, indexes)?
- What prefixes, roots, or suffixes can give me a clue about the word's meaning?
- Does this word look or sound like any other words with which I am familiar?
- Are there any parts of the word I already know?
- What words from my everyday speech could I swap with other words to make the sentence easier to follow?
- How can looking at the way the word is used in the sentence help me make a good guess about what the word means?

CHAPTER 6

- Are there other words around the one I don't know that will help me guess at a meaning?
- Is there a definition of the word given in the sentence? (Definitions often follow commas, such as "Twitter, an online social network, allows people to communicate using 140 characters.")

PIE CHART VOCABULARY

Below is a pie chart for an activity your instructor might choose to have you do in class as a vocabulary self-assessment tool. You will also need two different colored highlighters, markers, or colored pencils for this activity.

Your instructor will give you a list of up to twenty vocabulary words along with brief definitions and/or synonyms (words with similar meanings). During the activity, number the sections of the pie chart according to the number of vo-

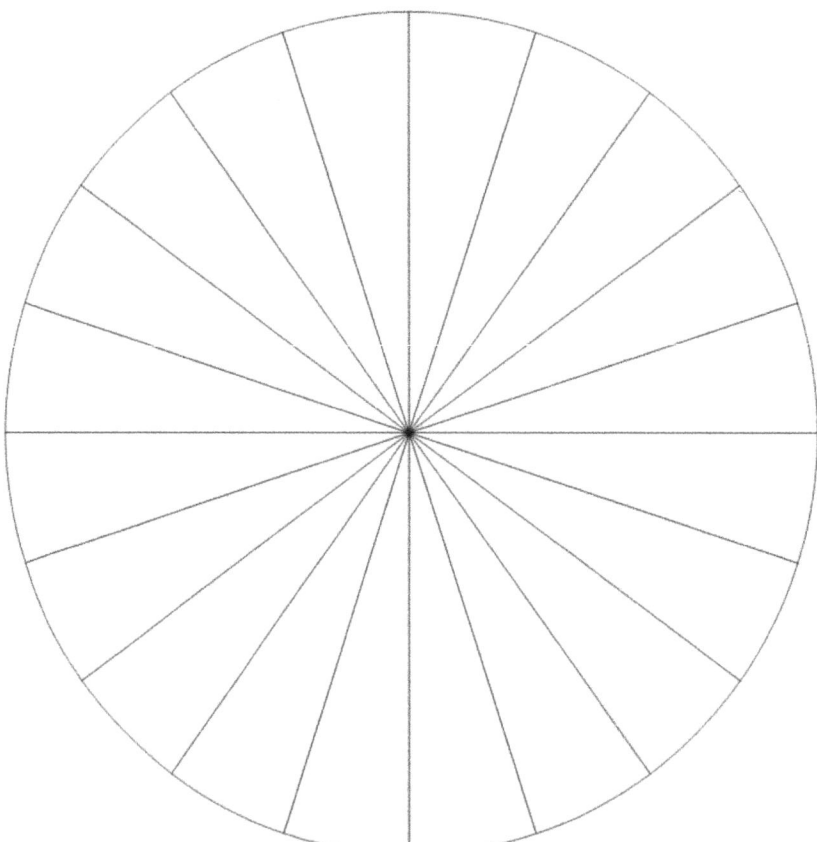

Figure 6.1. Pie Chart Vocabulary

cabulary words, and then write the words and definitions/synonyms around the outside edges of the chart.

Designate one of the colors you have available as "I know this word" and the other as "I need to study this word." Based on your own assessment of how well you know the meaning of each word, fill in the corresponding section on the pie chart with one color or the other.

When you are finished, look at your chart to see how the colors reveal the gaps in your vocabulary knowledge. You can easily use the chart and the jotted-in definitions/synonyms to study the words you don't know well.

WAYS TO STUDY LISTS OF TERMS

- The sooner you review vocabulary or word parts, the more likely you are to remember them. As soon as class dismisses and you leave the classroom, step to the side of the hall and review your list, or as soon as you get into your car or dorm room, review your list.
- You have a greater chance of remembering information if you write it down, even if you throw the paper away.
- The human brain can pay full attention for about twenty minutes. The key is to study often for short periods of time, not once or twice for long periods of time. Cramming doesn't work.
- The last time you study should be right before going to sleep when less stimuli from the day is coming in to cloud your intake of information.
- Vary the way you study from lists. The brain remembers more of what was encountered first, so avoid always starting at the top. Sometimes start at the top and work down. Other times start at the bottom and work up. And other times, start in the middle.
- Tape the list of terms or word parts somewhere you always look, so you have many encounters with the information. Consider putting the list on the mirror where you brush your teeth, on the fridge door, and so forth.
- Set the clock on your phone or other device for alerts to remind you to take out your list for a fifteen-minute study session.
- Upload flash card or vocabulary apps for quick and easy reviews when you have just a few minutes to spare.
- Use hard copy or electronic versions of index cards. Write or type the word or word part in one color on one side and the meaning in another color on the other side.

Number Prefixes		
Prefixes	**Meaning**	**Example**
Uni	One	Universe
Bi	Two	Binary
Tri	Three	Triangle
Tetra, quad	Four	Quadrant, quadrilateral
Penta, quinta, quin	Five	Pentagon
Sex, hex, hexa	Six	Hexagon
Hepta, hep, sept	Seven	Heptagon
Octa, octo, oct	Eight	Octopus
Nov	Nine	Novena
Deca, dec	Ten	Decade, decagon

Math & Science Roots & Affixes		
Roots & Affixes	**Meaning**	**Example**
De	Down	Descend or decrease
Dia	Through	Diagonal, diagram
Dyna	Power	Dynamic
Equa	Equal	Equate, equator
Ex	Out	Exit, exponents
Fract	Break	Fraction, fracture
Geo	Earth	Geology
Gon	Side	Polygon
Hydro	Water	Hydrate, hydroponic
Inter	Between	Interact, internal
Intra	Within	Intravenous
Junct	Join	Junction
Magni	Great, big	Magnify
Ology	Study of	Geology, biology
Para	Beside	Parallel, parabola
Poly	Many	Polynomials
Pre	Before	Precede
Prime	First	Primer, primitive
Therm	Heat	Thermometer
Vert	Turn	Vertical, vertex

7

CREATING VISUALS TO ENHANCE COMPREHENSION AND RECALL

I am a visual thinker, not a language-based thinker. My brain is like Google images.

—Temple Grandin

> **Point to ponder:** Think about why information taken in through a visual image is easier to remember than information taken in through listening to someone talk or through reading words on a page.

PRACTICE CREATING VISUALS

Read through the short text, "Classic Scientific Management Theory." As you go along, create at least one visual (picture, diagram, chart, etc.) for each paragraph to illustrate the points being made. For instance, you might draw a short timeline of the theory's development or a beehive to illustrate factory workers. A box in which to draw your visuals has been provided below the article. There are five paragraphs, so you should create at least five visuals.

Illustrate the parts that will best help you remember the basic characteristics of the classic scientific management theory.

CHAPTER 7

CLASSIC SCIENTIFIC MANAGEMENT THEORY

Classic scientific management theory came about in the late 1800s and has had a great impact on American business, especially manufacturing. It is called scientific because it is based on studying work processes to increase economic effectiveness and worker productivity and to decrease waste of materials, labor, and time.

The theory was initially developed in the 1880s by a man named Frederick Winslow Taylor, who began investigating labor processes of that period. Through the 1890s up to around 1910, the theory was further developed and began to have a significant impact on the manufacturing industry. Its influence peaked in the decade leading up to 1920 and then leveled out as competing theories arose. By the 1930s, the popularity of Taylor's theory had faded significantly, but its influence on industry has remained.

A main aspect of classic scientific management theory is what has become known as the division of labor, in which larger tasks are divided into smaller, more specialized ones. Individual workers perform these more specialized tasks repetitively as steps in a process to develop a product or to complete a project or work assignment. Managers closely supervise workers to ensure quality and productivity.

Factory assembly lines are an obvious example of this. However, many offices, especially bureaucracies, can be organized according to this theory, with workers often in cubicles performing narrowly specified jobs overseen by various levels of management.

Whether in the factory or the office, focus tends to be on the organization as a whole rather than on the individual workers. Workers are trained to follow precise directions to complete a task. Independent thinking or decision making is not generally encouraged, nor are workers invited to give input into the company's operation. Instead, managers make decisions based on what will benefit the organization overall, such as policies that will cut costs and raise productivity levels.

CREATING VISUALS TO ENHANCE COMPREHENSION AND RECALL

Figure 7.1. Box for Visuals

Without looking back at your drawings, write a summary of the classic scientific management theory. As you write, think about the visuals you drew and the sequence in which you drew them.

_____
_____
_____
_____
_____
_____
_____
_____
_____

CHAPTER 7

_____

_____

_____

_____

_____

When you've completed writing the summary, return to your drawings and the text to check the accuracy of your memory.

8

KEEPING IT REAL

Education is not the learning of facts, but the training of the mind to think.
—Albert Einstein

> **Point to ponder:** Think about how vital it is to not only be able to comprehend what you read in today's world, but to be able to effectively put that information to use.

PROFESSIONAL SPOTLIGHT INTERVIEWS

Read through the interviews of the two professionals below to see how strong reading skills are vital in their chosen careers.

Professional Spotlight Reading Interview with Kenneth Seel

Title: marriage and family therapist and certified alcohol and drug counselor
Location: Jackson, Michigan

Amelia: Could you talk about your experiences with reading?

Ken: I was a very, very poor student in school. I got the reputation that I was one of the dummies. They just passed that along as I went through school. When I

CHAPTER 8

Figure 8.1. Ken Seel

graduated from high school, I was going to join the military, but it was the Vietnam War, and a friend of mine, actually the father of the lady I was dating, suggested that probably was not a good idea, people getting killed and what not. He encouraged me to go to junior college. I thought, "I'll never go to junior college. I graduated with a D average," but he told me he could help me get in.

My biggest problem was I couldn't read. When they tested me, I actually read at about a fourth-grade level. I basically couldn't read at all. Since I enjoyed sailing and scuba diving and things like that, this man found magazines and books like that, things that interested me, and he got me to read them. That's how I got started reading. Then he also gave me storybooks and paperback books to read.

He also told me what to do when I was in class. One was taking very copious notes, and then at the end of every chapter of every book, they would always have something like twenty questions of things you needed to know. I'd answer all those questions, and then I tape recorded everything. That's how I studied. Everything I had, all my studying, was done on tape. I even carried that through when I went into grad school years later. All my notes, everything that I had to study, I always put it on tape. Because when I listened to it, I could get it better than when I read it.

Amelia: Were you actually reading the text aloud into the tape recorder and then listening to it later?

Ken: No. I'd read the book, but especially in junior college, it was very difficult to understand things I was reading. I had to listen in class, write down notes, then read them into the tape recorder, and then take those questions at the end of the book and answer them the best I could. I'd have to keep skimming back in the book and try to find the answers. But I got into the habit of reading.

Later, I lived in the Caribbean for years and there wasn't TV, and I lived on boats a lot. The only recreation I had was reading. So to this day, I always have two books going constantly. I'll have some junk novel I'm reading but also some psychology book or something, and I read every night before I go to bed. When I'm hanging out at the house, that's what I do; I read a lot.

Amelia: So actually the more reading you did the better you got at it?

Ken: That's how I learned to read, by reading.

Amelia: How much reading do you think is required in your type of profession as an alcohol and drug counselor?

Ken: Every day when I teach groups, they have process notes they fill out. I have to read those and make my notes. So there's a lot of reading and writing. We do assessments. So I sit down and talk to people, and I have to type the information about their history. So there's a lot to do. There's a lot of reading. And then any information about any new idea or new technique or just basic information about the drug and alcohol field or psychology field is found in books. You have to read it and read articles.

Amelia: If you could estimate in percentages, how much of the reading material you look at is online vs. hard copy?

Ken: Most of it is books. Now, when it comes to work-related material, probably about half and half. When it comes to recreational reading, I still like books.

Amelia: If you were thinking about people who were fresh out of college, what kinds of challenges do you think they might encounter going into your field if they were struggling readers?

Ken: Well, there's a lot of paperwork to do when you're in this business. It takes up a good deal of time. And if you have problems reading, it's just going to slow you down. Every time I teach a class with fourteen or fifteen people in it, at the end of that class, I have to read their progress notes and write my assessments. There's a lot of paperwork to be done, and if you're a slow reader or have difficulty reading, it can be a problem.

Amelia: When you say "class," you mean groups of incarcerated people who are taking classes you conduct?

Ken: Yes, I facilitate groups whether they're process groups or didactic groups. The point is that when you're done with these groups, there are notes to be written and forms to be filled out, and it takes a lot of time. If you're a poor reader, it's going to get in the way.

Professional Spotlight Reading Interview with Jason Brinker

Title: technical services supervisor for an IT/software company
Location: College Station, Texas

Amelia: What type of reading is required the most in your profession?

Jason: In my job, there is a lot of technical documentation required. We need to read manuals for a myriad of different IT products as well as different protocols for our business IT service.

Amelia: When you're doing this technical reading, what is the length? Are you talking about small chunks, pages and pages, or chapters and chapters?

Jason: If I know specifically what I'm looking for, I can typically jump right to it in the technical manual for the equipment I use. However, if I don't know exactly what we're looking to do or the capabilities of the equipment they want to use, it could be ten to fifteen pages, but not past fifteen.

Amelia: You said if it's something you're familiar with, you can kind of skip and jump in where you need to. How do you determine what's important enough to look at and what isn't?

Jason: It's my experience. When I'm dealing with equipment and I'm reading through a technical manual, they want to tell me about why the feature is in there

Figure 8.2. Jason Brinker

and how it can save me money, things like that. I don't care. I really just need to know about the feature. I basically weed out the sales pitch.

Amelia: How do you do that? Do you skim through the reading, see things like that, and then skip them?

Jason: Yeah, I just skim things usually.

Amelia: And then you just move on?

Jason: Yep.

Amelia: How do you go about thinking through the vital information to understand what you are reading?

Jason: In a typical situation, I'm given a task. That task could be to find a product to research to determine if it fits into our business needs. I know how our software is delivered to the end user, and I use that knowledge to look through the capabilities of the equipment I'm researching to be sure the product will work. I make sure it supports the multiple protocols or fulfills a particular function, and then I read through the documentation to determine ease of use. In an IT business, the little details need to be taken into account on all products, and I always re-read to make sure I didn't miss something that could affect my end purpose.

Amelia: If there are students coming out of college with degrees, but they aren't proficient readers, could they still qualify for a job working with you? If so, how would they get around the reading deficit?

Jason: That's more of a management question in terms of if they will be hired if they're not proficient in technical reading. I won't necessarily have that expectation when they first get hired on, but it will be something I expect them to learn by experience. I will see to that personally. I will tell them to go find this particular feature in the manual, and I'll make them do that. When I tell my guys to go find something, they know I don't like them to just regurgitate information. I don't want a definition. I want an *operational* definition. I want them to understand how it works. That can only come from doing the research and reading through the manual. So there are two things my guys know. They'll put them on my gravestone. "Get better, faster" and "Give me an *operational* definition; don't just give me a definition."

Amelia: Let's say someone gets hired and you give them some opportunities to go find operational definitions and they can't do it. Would you find ways to remediate or would you dismiss them?

Jason: That's a tough question because I like to believe everybody can learn, and I've yet to find anybody I couldn't teach. But quite honestly, I wouldn't have much use for them if they couldn't do it. It's so important. I would expect it to be a daily function of their job. They would have to learn how to do it. If they couldn't, I'd look to see if there was another position somewhere else and move them out.

Amelia: It sounds like it would be labor intensive to teach someone when you probably have a host of other candidates who are more able to do that.

Jason: Yeah. It would be great if I took a guy who came right out of school, for instance, and he could do exactly what I told him if I said, "Use this wire. Look at this protocol. I want you to tell me how it works." I'd want him to come back and give me everything I was looking for and say, "It works like this. This piece of equipment works. Here's an alternative from the same vendor. We can use this." That's a huge part of training that I wouldn't have to do. I would definitely consider him over somebody who couldn't do that. Unfortunately I don't get to give them a technical reading test before they get hired at my company.

Amelia: How are people generally hired?

Jason: Most of the people who work for me have been promoted into the position. I don't hire them off the street. Not that we wouldn't. It's just that we haven't found any candidates we could. They'd have to start somewhere else in the company, get some experience, and then be moved into that position.

Amelia: If students are coming to you straight out of school, where would they start?

Jason: Some have started in phone support. Somebody calls in and says, "I need to do this, my printer doesn't work, or my router doesn't work." It's in that position someone hired in would start learning technical reading skills. We write our own manuals. So they're reading these manuals while assisting someone over the phone. I've got two people who started out like that. Right off the bat, they're learning technical reading.

Amelia: Are there tests for people hired in those jobs?

Jason: We have another company that tests first. They run a whole testing scope where they test technical knowledge, comprehension, how quick someone is to learn. I don't think it has a technical reading side of it. It doesn't especially test for that.

Amelia: When you hired in, how did you learn technical reading? Did you have these skills from school? How did you get to the point where you are now?

Jason: I have the ability to remember about 90 percent of what I read. It's kind of one of those things that come naturally to me, but I do want to say I learned quite a bit more on the job than in school. There have been some times it was kind of rough. I was trying to figure out what I was reading. Trying to figure out something in a technical manual is boring. I would always get distracted. Now I can go through that tech manual, find where I need to be, find what I'm looking for, and have the answer.

Amelia: Is it because you're now familiar with it? If you switched jobs, would you struggle again?

Jason: No. I've learned how to do it now. Also, we look at so many pieces of standard equipment. If I switch companies and they ask me to look at something, there's a very good possibility I will already know how it works or be able to quickly figure it out.

Amelia: Is there anything you wish you'd known before you got the job that you think college students should know?

Jason: I think probably the biggest thing is if they're going into an IT company, that's what their degree is in, they need to learn to read technical manuals and comprehend them quickly. The number one thing that would be helpful is some kind of way to stay on task. It is boring to read through tech manuals, and your mind starts to wander unless you're super interested in it or if you have a specific goal to look for something. I mean that was my only thing; it's just boring. You need some kind of exercise when you're reading to keep your mind on task.

Amelia: So your mind wanders if it's boring and you don't have a specific purpose for reading?

Jason: Yeah. If I'm looking for a certain protocol that works with a specific router, that always helps me stay focused, or if I'm looking for a specific item or I'm trying to learn how to do something and I need to learn how to do it. Probably one of the most important things in my profession is reading with a goal. If you can read with a goal in mind and keep your mind engaged, you'll pick up on it really fast. I talk to my guys and their biggest complaint is they read something three times because they keep getting distracted.

CONDUCT YOUR OWN PROFESSIONAL READING INTERVIEW

Use the following questions to interview some professional people to find out how important reading skills are to their chosen careers.

1. How important are strong reading skills in your profession?
2. What type of reading is required most often?
3. How do you determine what to focus on when you are reading?
4. Do you use any particular strategies to get through challenging material?
5. Were you always a good reader or is that something you developed in college or later in your career?
6. What helped you become skilled at reading?
7. Is there anything that you know about reading now that you wish you had known in college?
8. If there are students coming out of college with degrees but they aren't proficient readers, could they still qualify for a job working in your field? If so, how would they get around the reading deficits?

www.ingramcontent.com/pod-product-compliance
Ingram Content Group UK Ltd.
Pitfield, Milton Keynes, MK11 3LW, UK
UKHW050007230326
469204UK00010B/328